BUSY BEES
SUMMER

Fun for Two's and Three's

By Elizabeth McKinnon and Gayle Bittinger
Illustrated by Barb Tourtillotte

Totline
PUBLICATIONS

Warren Publishing House
A Division of Frank Schaffer Publications
Torrance, California

We wish to thank the following teachers, childcare workers, and parents for contributing some of the ideas in this book: Pat Beck, Red Lion, PA; Brian Biddinger, Orlando, FL; Nancy Nason Biddinger, Orlando, FL; Janice Bodenstedt, Jackson, MI; Karen Brown, Dry Ridge, KY; Mildred Claus, Parma, OH; Patricia Coyne, Mansfield, MA; Frank Dally, Ankeny, IA; Cindy Dingwall, Palatine, IL; Gina Duddy, Arlington, MA; Linda Ferguson, Olympia, WA; Paula C. Foreman, Lancaster, PA; Judy Hall, Wytheville, VA; Gemma Hall-Hart, Bellingham, WA; Johanne Hooker, Glendale, AZ; JoAnn C. Leist, Smithfield, NC; Debra Lindahl, Libertyville, IL; Kathy McCullough, St. Charles, IL; Susan A. Miller, Kutztown, PA; Susan Nydick, Philadelphia, PA; Susan M. Paprocki, Northbrook, IL; Barbara Paxson, Champion, OH; Susan Peters, Upland, CA; Dawn Picolelli, Wilmington, DE; Lois E. Putnam, Pilot Mountain, NC; Beverly Qualheim, Marquette, MI; Polly Reedy, Elmhurst, IL; Betty Silkunas, Lansdale, PA; Carla Cotter Skjong, Tyler, MN; Diane Thom, Maple Valley, WA; Mary Ulrich, Gilbertsville, PA; Becky Valenick, Rockford, IL; Barbara Vilet, Cortland, IL; Kristine Wagoner, Puyallup, WA; Cynthia Walters, Mechanicsburg, PA.

Editorial Staff:
Managing Editor: Kathleen Cubley
Editors: Susan Hodges, Jean Warren
Copy Editor and Proofreader: Kris Fulsaas
Editorial Assistants: Kate Ffolliott, Erica West

Design and Production Staff:
Art Managers: Uma Kukathas, Jill Lustig
Book Design: Lynne Faulk
Layout Production: Gordon Frazier
Cover Design: Brenda Mann Harrison
Cover Illustration: Barb Tourtillotte
Busy Bee Drawings: Susan Dahlman
Production Manager: JoAnna Brock

ISBN 1-57029-066-0

Library of Congress Catalog Number 94-61734
Printed in the United States of America
Published by: Warren Publishing House

Editorial Office: P.O. Box 2250
Everett, WA 98203

Business Office: 23740 Hawthorne Blvd.
Torrance, CA 90505

20 19 18 17 16 15 14 13 12 11 10 9 8 7 6 5 4 3

INTRODUCTION

Welcome to the Summer edition of *Busy Bees—Fun for Two's and Three's*, an idea resource for teachers and parents of children 2 through 3 years old.

Busy Bees—Fun for Two's and Three's offers age-appropriate, fun, attention-getting activities. It is filled with hands-on projects and movement games that are just right for busy little ones. Also included are language and snack suggestions suitable for two's and three's, plus a rhyme and one or more songs to accompany each chapter.

The ideas in this book are designed to complement your everyday curriculum. The chapters are listed in an order that you may wish to follow day by day, although each one stands alone and can be used in a pick-and-choose fashion. You will find that the activities are perfect for those times when you want to interject group participation and purposefulness into your usual free-play agenda.

We hope that the suggestions in *Busy Bees—Fun for Two's and Three's* will act as a catalyst and inspire you to add ideas and activities of your own to those in the book.

Happy teaching!

CONTENTS

August

JUNE

Water

Exploring Water

Fill plastic dishpans with warm water. Add water-play toys such as those listed below and encourage your children to use them for pouring, squeezing, squirting, and sprinkling.

- plastic measuring cups
- plastic funnels
- sponges
- plastic squeeze bottles
- kitchen basters
- plastic containers with holes punched around the bottoms

MOVEMENT

Making Bubbles

Fill a basin or a large tub with water. Let your children take turns standing by the basin, spreading their fingers, then rapidly moving their hands back and forth in the water to make bubbles.

RHYME

Water, Water

Water, water
Everywhere,
On my face
And on my hair,
On my fingers,
On my toes.
Water, water
On my nose!

Jean Warren

SONG

Water Song

Sung to: "The Wheels on the Bus"

Oh, the water
In the cup goes
Splash, splash, splash.
Splash, splash, splash.
Splash, splash, splash.
Oh, the water
In the cup goes
Splash, splash, splash
When I pour it out.

Oh, the water
In the bottle goes
Squirt, squirt, squirt.
Squirt, squirt, squirt.
Squirt, squirt, squirt.
Oh, the water
In the bottle goes
Squirt, squirt, squirt
When I squeeze it out.

Additional verse: Oh, the water in the sponge goes drip, drip, drip when I squish it out.

Jean Warren

LANGUAGE IDEA

Talk with your children about different ways we use water such as for drinking, cooking, bathing, washing clothes, and watering plants.

SNACK IDEA

Let your children help mix water with juice concentrate to make a snacktime drink.

Wading Pools

Fill It Up

Place an inflatable plastic wading pool on the ground outdoors. Using a garden hose, let your children help fill the pool with water. Then add water toys for the children to play with in the pool.

Variation: For an indoor activity, place an empty wading pool on the floor and let your children fill it with pillows.

MOVEMENT

Splish, Splash

Let your children take turns standing in a water-filled wading pool and splashing with their hands and feet.

Variation: Let your children stand in an empty pool and pretend to splash.

RHYME

Our Wading Pool

Let's fill up
Our wading pool
With water
From the hose.
Then we'll make
Some splashes
With our fingers
And our toes!

Elizabeth McKinnon

Let's Go Wading

Sung to: "Frere Jacques"

Let's go wading,
Let's go wading
In our pool,
In our pool.
Splishy-splashy
Splish, splash.
Splishy-splashy
Splish, splash.
Feels so cool,
Feels so cool.

Elizabeth McKinnon

LANGUAGE IDEA

Have your children gather around a small wading pool. Give them directions to follow such as these: "Put one hand in the pool. Put in two hands. Step inside the pool. Now step outside it. Walk around the pool. Now crawl around it."

SNACK IDEA

Serve a snack poolside, either indoors or out.

Floating and Sinking

Sink or Float?

Set out a water-filled dishpan. Collect several objects that float, such as a sponge, a cork, and a rubber ball, and several objects that sink such as a rock, a crayon, and a metal spoon. Hold up one object at a time and ask your children to guess whether it will sink or float. Then let them place the object in the water to see if their guesses were correct.

MOVEMENT

Like a Rock

Play music and let your children pretend to be boats, rubber ducks, or similar objects floating around in the water. Whenever you stop the music, have the children pretend to be rocks and sink to the floor.

RHYME

What Do You Think?

If a leaf
Falls in water,
What do you
Think?
Will the
Leaf float
Or will the
Leaf sink?

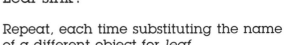

Repeat, each time substituting the name of a different object for *leaf*.

Elizabeth McKinnon

SONG

Sink and Float Song

Sung to: "Clementine"

Find a rock,
Find a rock,
Find a rock
Right now.
Put the rock
In the water.
Put it in
The water now.

Watch it sink,
Watch it sink,
Watch it sink
Right now.
Watch it sink
In the water.
Watch it sink
Right now.

Repeat, substituting the word *sponge* for *rock* and *float* for *sink*. Continue with similar verses about other objects that sink and float.

Elizabeth McKinnon

LANGUAGE IDEA

Set out objects that float and objects that sink. Make up a story about the objects as your children take turns dropping them into a tub of water.

SNACK IDEA

Serve soup with vegetables or noodles that sink and let your children float small crackers on top.

Sandals

Sandal Match

Find different kinds and sizes of sandals and place several pairs in a box. Let your children take turns sorting through the sandals to find the matching pairs. Occasionally add another pair to make the game more challenging.

MOVEMENT

Sandal Walk

Set out different kinds of sandals in large sizes. Let your children take turns trying on the sandals and walking around the room in them.

RHYME

My Sandal Shoes

My sandal shoes
Are reddish brown,
With airy holes
All around.
And when it is
A nice warm day,
I wear my sandals
Out to play.

Lois E. Putnam

Sandals

Sung to: "If You're Happy and You Know It"

Sandals keep
Our feet so cool,
Oh, so cool.
Sandals keep
Our feet so cool,
Oh, so cool.
Sandals keep
Our feet so cool
When we play
At home or school.
Sandals keep
Our feet so cool,
Oh, so cool.

Elizabeth McKinnon

LANGUAGE IDEA

Talk with your children about how sandals are like ordinary shoes and how they are different.

SNACK IDEA

Let your children wear sandals while they eat their snack.

Buckets

HANDS-ON LEARNING GAME

Nesting Fun

Collect three or four plastic buckets that will fit one inside the other. Show your children how to nest the buckets. Then take the buckets apart and let the children take turns nesting them.

MOVEMENT

Bucket Lift

Place empty buckets on the floor. Ask your children to pretend that the buckets are full of rocks and have them show how they would lift the buckets. Continue by having the children pretend that the buckets are full of other materials such as feathers, bricks, cotton balls, or sand.

RHYME

A Bucket

Here is a bucket
To carry about.
Fill it way up,
Then empty it out.

Elizabeth McKinnon

Bucket Song

Sung to: "Ten Little Indians"

Shovel in the sand,
Fill up your bucket.
Shovel in the sand,
Fill up your bucket.
Shovel in the sand,
Fill up your bucket.
Fill up your bucket now.

Dump out the sand,
Empty your bucket.
Dump out the sand,
Empty your bucket.
Dump out the sand,
Empty your bucket.
Empty your bucket now.

Repeat, each time substituting a
different word, such as *blocks* or *dirt*,
for *sand*.

Elizabeth McKinnon

LANGUAGE IDEA

Hide a familiar object inside a
bucket. Describe the object and
let your children try to guess
what it is.

SNACK IDEA

Wrap snack foods in aluminum
foil or plastic wrap. Serve them to
your children from a clean
bucket.

Sand

Exploring Sand

Set out a dishpan of sand for each of your children. Provide sand-play toys such as those listed below and let the children use them for digging, scooping, pouring, and sifting.

- small shovels or spoons
- scoops
- plastic measuring cups
- plastic funnels
- plastic containers
- sifters

Extension: Let your children play in damp sand with cookie cutters or sand molds.

MOVEMENT

Digging With Feet

Designate a special time in your sand area for "feet-only" digging. Have your children take off their shoes and socks. Then let them dig, design, and build with their bare feet.

RHYME

Sand Everywhere

Sand on the beach.
Sand on the doll.
Sand on the pail.
Sand on the ball.

Sand on the blanket.
Sand on the bear.
Sand on the shovel.
Sand everywhere!

Jean Warren

SONG

I Love Sand

Sung to: "Three Blind Mice"

Sand, sand, sand.
Sand, sand, sand.
I love sand.
I love sand.
It's fun to squish it
Between my toes,
Or build a mountain
As high as my nose,
Or dig a tunnel
That grows and grows,
'Cause I love sand!

Susan Hodges

LANGUAGE IDEA

Bury small toys or other familiar objects in sand. Let your children dig them up and name them.

SNACK IDEA

Thoroughly wash and dry some of your sand molds and use them for making gelatin.

Scooping

HANDS-ON LEARNING GAME

Sand Scoops

Use clean plastic bleach bottles or laundry detergent bottles to make Sand Scoops for your children. To make each one, squeeze glue around the opening of the bottle and tightly screw on the lid. Then use a craft knife to cut off the bottom of the bottle at an angle. Smooth over any rough edges. Let the children play with their scoops in sand, experimenting to see how many scoops it takes to fill various containers.

MOVEMENT

Scooping Moves

Have your children pretend to scoop up different materials using various sizes of make-believe scoops. For example, ask them to use tiny scoops to scoop up imaginary beads or giant scoops to scoop up pretend feather pillows.

RHYME

Here Is My Scoop

Here is my scoop.
Watch me go.
I scoop up the sand
Just like so.
>   (Make scooping motions.)

Repeat, each time substituting a different word, such as *peas* or *dirt*, for *sand*.

Elizabeth McKinnon

SONG

Scoop and Count

Sung to: "Row, Row, Row Your Boat"

Scoop, scoop,
Scoop the sand.
Scoop it,
One, two, three.
Scooping, scooping,
Scooping, scooping,
Scoop and count
With me.

Repeat, each time substituting a different word, such as *beans* or *dirt*, for *sand*.

Elizabeth McKinnon

LANGUAGE IDEA

Place small objects on the floor and set out scoops. Give your children directions such as these: "Scoop up something red. Scoop up a toy. Scoop up something that bounces."

SNACK IDEA

Pour dry cereal into a large bowl. Let your children scoop out the cereal into smaller bowls to eat for a snack.

Shells

---HANDS-ON LEARNING GAME---

Shell Play

Collect various kinds and sizes of sea shells. Bury the shells in a tub of sand and let your children dig through the sand to find them. When all the shells have been found, have the children line them up from smallest to largest or from largest to smallest.

---MOVEMENT---

Open Shells, Closed Shells

Let your children pretend to be clams living in the sea. When you call out, "Clams, open your shells!" have the children stretch their arms out at their sides. When you call out, "Clams, close your shells!" have the children raise their arms high overhead, fingers touching. Continue calling out directions as long as interest lasts.

---RHYME---

Sea Shells

See the pretty
Sea shells.
Count them
One by one.
Line them up
Upon the sand.
It really is
Quite fun!

Adapted Traditional

SONG

Pretty Sea Shell

Sung to: "Frere Jacques"

Pretty sea shell,
Pretty sea shell
On the sand,
On the sand.
Pick it up
And hold it,
Pick it up
And hold it
In your hand,
In your hand.

Elizabeth McKinnon

LANGUAGE IDEA

Sit with your children and pass around a sea shell. Encourage them to describe what the shell looks and feels like.

SNACK IDEA

Cook pasta shells and use them to make soup or salad at snacktime.

Fish

Fish Mural

Cut fish shapes out of white construction paper. Let your children decorate the shapes with crayons or felt-tip markers. Help the children glue their fish shapes onto a piece of butcher paper. Add twisted green crepe-paper streamers for seaweed. Then hang the butcher paper on a wall and cover it with blue cellophane to make an underwater scene.

MOVEMENT

Swimming Fishes

Have your children imagine that they are little fishes. Play music and let them "swim" around the room, swishing their pretend tails as they go.

RHYME

Fishies

Fishies, fishies,
Swimming round,
Sometimes up,
Sometimes down,
Sometimes fast,
Sometimes slow.
Near the net
We'd better not go!

Kathy McCullough

SONG

Fish, Fish

Sung to: "Skip to My Lou"

Fish, fish,
Swim up high.
Fish, fish,
Swim down low.
Fish, fish,
Swim so fast,
Fish, fish,
Swim so slow.

Have your children act out the movements as you sing the song.

Betty Silkunas

LANGUAGE IDEA

Glue small pictures onto fish shapes and place them in a box. As your children "fish" for the shapes, incorporate the pictures into a story you make up.

SNACK IDEA

Serve your children fish-shaped crackers for a snack.

Crabs

HANDS-ON LEARNING GAME

Learning About Five

Hold up a picture of a crab. Help your children count five legs on one side of the crab and five legs on the other side. Then make sets of five with the children, using objects such as blocks, crayons, or toy cars.

MOVEMENT

Crab Walk

Have your children pretend to be little crabs on a sandy beach. Encourage them to crawl around sideways, first going one way, then the other. (Explain that sideways is the only way that crabs can move.)

RHYME

A Crab

Along the beach
By the sea,
Search
As you go by.
   (Cup hand above eye.)
If you look
Quite carefully,
A crab
You'll surely spy.
   (Move hands like crab claws.)

Susan Peters

SONG

Saw a Crab

Sung to: "Clementine"

I went walking,
I went walking,
Saw a crab
Right on the beach.
Saw a crab,
Saw a crab
Walking this way
With its feet.
   (Walk sideways.)

Cindy Dingwall

LANGUAGE IDEA

Set out a crab cutout and several different rocks. Let your children take turns following directions such as these: "Put the crab on top of the biggest rock. Put the crab under the black rock. Put the crab beside the round rock."

SNACK IDEA

Encourage your children to use their thumbs and fingers like crab pincers when they eat their snack.

Rub-A-Dub-Dub

Three Men in a Tub

Give each of your children a margarine tub to decorate with stickers. Inside their tubs, let them each place three items, such as spools, film canisters, or small cardboard tubes, to represent three men in a tub. Then let the children float their tubs in dishpans filled with water.

MOVEMENT

Circle Game

Form a "tub" by holding hands with your children in a circle. Have three of the children stand in the middle to represent three men in a tub. Walk around them in a circle as everyone recites the rhyme "Rub-A-Dub-Dub" (this page). Then choose three other children to stand in the middle and start the game again.

RHYME

Rub-A-Dub-Dub

Rub-a-dub-dub,
Three men in a tub.
And who do you think
They be?
The butcher, the baker,
The candlestick maker.
Helpers they are,
All three.

Adapted Traditional

In a Tub

Sung to: "Frere Jacques"

Butcher, baker,
Candlestick maker
In a tub.
Rub-a-dub-dub.
Floating round
This way,
Floating round
That way
In their tub.
Rub-a-dub-dub.

Elizabeth McKinnon

LANGUAGE IDEA

Recite the rhyme "Rub-A-Dub-Dub" (page 28), each time substituting a different word, such as *toy-car maker, ice cream maker,* or *crayon maker,* for *candlestick maker.*

SNACK IDEA

At snacktime, serve meat from the "butcher" and bread from the "baker." Place unlighted candles in holders on the table from the "candlestick maker."

Jobs

Job Fun

Set out hats and other props used by various kinds of workers such as firefighters, police officers, construction workers, chefs, clowns, and baseball players. Let your children try on the hats and use the props as they pretend to do different jobs.

MOVEMENT

Worker Moves

Have your children pretend to be workers as you take the part of their boss. Lead them in doing various kinds of jobs such as fighting a fire, directing traffic, building a house, or making bread.

RHYME

Our Country's Workers

We work in the factories
And in the offices too.
We are the workers
All around you.

We work at the post office
And we work at the zoo.
Truckers, teachers, builders—
We work hard for you.

Brian Biddinger
Nancy Nason Biddinger

What Will You Be?

Sung to: "The Wheels on the Bus"

What will you be
When you grow up,
You grow up,
You grow up?
What will you be
When you grow up,
When you're older?

Jacob's going to be
A firefighter,
Firefighter,
Firefighter.
Jacob's going to be
A firefighter
When he's older.

Sing the song for each of your children,
substituting the child's name for *Jacob*
and what he or she wants to be for
firefighter.

Frank Dally

Name several things that a par-
ticular worker does such as bake
bread, make cookies, and frost
cakes. Then ask your children to
guess the worker's job (a baker).

Give each of your children a job
to do to prepare for snacktime.
Include setting the table, making
the snack, and cleaning up
afterward.

Boats

Color Boat Match

Cut identical boat shapes and sail shapes out of three different colors of felt. Place the boat shapes on a flannelboard. Give the sail shapes to your children and let them take turns placing the sails above the matching-colored boats.

MOVEMENT

Over the Waves We Go

Have your children pretend to be sitting in a large rowboat. Sit at the front of the pretend boat and show the children how to "row" all together as the waves rock you back and forth. Then lead the children in paddling a big canoe.

RHYME

Little Boat

Look in the
Toy box.
Find a
Little boat.
Put it
In the water
And watch
It float.

Elizabeth McKinnon

Rowing

Sung to: "Row, Row, Row Your Boat"

Waves, waves,
Back and forth,
Rock the boat
All day.
    (Move hands like waves.)
We row and row
So we can go
Somewhere
Far away.
    (Pretend to row boat.)

Jean Warren

LANGUAGE IDEA

Display pictures of different kinds of boats and ask your children to tell how they are alike and how they are different.

SNACK IDEA

Wrap snack foods in aluminum foil or plastic wrap and serve them from a large toy boat.

Trains

Cardboard-Box Train

Set out several cardboard boxes to use for train cars. Let your children decorate them by drawing on designs with crayons or felt-tip markers or by gluing on crepe-paper streamers. Line up the boxes, fasten them together with heavy yarn, and attach a yarn handle to the front box. Then let the children take turns pulling stuffed-animal "passengers" around the room in their decorated train.

MOVEMENT

Chugging Trains

Use pieces of masking tape to make railroad tracks on the floor. Let your children pretend to be trains and chug back and forth along the tracks while making choo-choo sounds.

RHYME

Clickety-Clack

Clickety-clack,
Clickety-clack.
See the train
On the track.

Clickety-clack,
Clickety-clack.
See the train
Going back.

Adapted Traditional

I'm a Little Red Train

Sung to: "Little White Duck"

I'm a little red train
Chugging down the track,
A little red train
Going up and back.
I travel all day
Going round and round,
Taking goods
From town to town.
I'm a little red train
Going down the track.
Chug, chug, chug.

Jean Warren

LANGUAGE IDEA

Tell a train story to your children. Whenever they hear the word *train*, have them say, "Choo-choo."

SNACK IDEA

Have your children pretend to be a train and chug in a line to the snack table.

Airplanes

Planes in Hangars

On a large piece of white paper, draw a red box, a yellow box, and a blue box to represent airplane hangars. Cut two airplane shapes each out of red, yellow, and blue construction paper. Mix up the shapes and let your children take turns placing the airplanes in the matching-colored hangars.

RHYME

In an Airplane

When I grow up
I'll say goodbye,
Then dart away
Into the sky.
I'll fly around
In my airplane,
But soon I will
Come down again.

Adapted Traditional

MOVEMENT

Zooming Airplanes

Let your children pretend to be airplanes. Have them hold their arms straight out at their sides and "fly" around the room while making zooming sounds. If desired, make a masking-tape runway on the floor for "takeoffs" and "landings."

LANGUAGE IDEA

Display a picture of an airplane and name its different parts with your children.

SNACK IDEA

Let your children sit in chairs lined up to resemble an airplane cabin. Serve snack foods on disposable food trays.

SONG

I'm an Airplane

Sung to: "Clementine"

I'm an airplane,
I'm an airplane
Flying up
Into the sky.
Flying higher,
Flying higher
As I watch
The clouds go by.

I'm an airplane,
I'm an airplane.
See me flying
All around.
Flying lower,
Flying lower
Till I land
Down on the ground.

Let your children act out the movements as you sing the song.

Elizabeth McKinnon

Doing the Wash

Washing Clothes

Pour warm water into dishpans and add small amounts of liquid dishwashing detergent. Set out a basket of "laundry" that includes items such as doll clothes, washcloths, or infant shirts and socks. Let your children take turns washing the laundry. When they have finished, dry the items in a dryer or hang them on a clothesline.

MOVEMENT

Washing Machines

Ask your children to imagine that they are washing machines. Walk among them, pretending to put in clothes and soap. When you "turn on" the machines, have them twist and shake until the imaginary clothes inside are all clean.

RHYME

Rub, Rub, Rub

Washing clothes,
Toss 'em in the tub.
Add some soap,
Then rub, rub, rub!

Elizabeth McKinnon

This Is the Way

Sung to: "The Mulberry Bush"

This is the way
We wash the clothes,
Wash the clothes,
Wash the clothes.
This is the way
We wash the clothes,
So early
In the morning.

Repeat, each time substituting a different word, such as *socks*, *shirts*, or *pants*, for *clothes*.

Traditional

LANGUAGE IDEA

Talk with your children about the steps in doing the wash, including sorting clothes, putting them into the washer, adding soap, and turning on the machine.

SNACK IDEA

Let your children help wash cloth placemats. Then dry the placemats and use them on the snack table.

Clothesline Fun

Hanging Up the Wash

Tie a clothesline between two short chairs. In a laundry basket, place items such as doll clothes, washcloths, or infant socks and shirts. Using slot-type clothespins, help your children hang up the items by kind (first all the socks, then all the shirts, etc.). Then help them hang up items by color or by number.

Bell Clothesline

Using pieces of yarn, hang small bells at various heights from an ordinary clothesline. Let your children take turns jumping and stretching to ring the bells.

On the Line

Wet clothes,
Wet clothes,
Hanging
On the line.
Let them
Dry
In the
Bright sunshine.

Repeat, each time substituting a different word, such as *socks* or *sheets*, for *clothes*.

Elizabeth McKinnon

SONG

On the Clothesline

Sung to: "My Bonnie Lies Over the Ocean"

Hang up the shirts
On the clothesline.
Oh, hang up the shirts
To dry.
Hang up the shirts
On the clothesline.
Oh, hang up the shirts
So high.
Hang up, hang up,
Oh, hang up the shirts
To dry, to dry.
Hang up, hang up,
Oh, hang up the shirts
So high.

Repeat, each time substituting a different word, such as *pants* or *towels*, for *shirts*.

Gayle Bittinger

LANGUAGE IDEA

Use slot-type clothespins to hang various items from a low clothesline. As you describe the different items, let your children remove them from the line.

SNACK IDEA

Place snack foods in resealable plastic sandwich bags. Clip the bags to a low clothesline to serve.

Sponges

HANDS-ON SCIENCE

Sponge Play

Pour warm water into dishpans and give your children a variety of dry sponges. Have the children put the sponges into the water. What happens to the sponges when they get wet? Encourage the children to experiment with squeezing and floating the sponges. Is there any way they can make the sponges sink? Can they make bubbles with the sponges?

MOVEMENT

Sponge Wipe

Let your children use damp or dry sponges to wipe various surfaces such as walls, tabletops, chair seats, or the floor. Encourage them to stretch their arms up and down and back and forth as they work.

RHYME

If I Had a Sponge

If I had
A little sponge
This is
What I'd do.
I'd wash the walls
And windows
And I'd scrub
The table, too.

Elizabeth McKinnon

SONG

I Wish I Had a Sponge

Sung to: "Twinkle, Twinkle, Little Star"

Oh, I wish
I had a sponge.
I know I'd have
Lots of fun.
I could wipe
And wipe all day.
I could squeeze it
When I play.
Oh, I wish
I had a sponge.
I know I'd have
Lots of fun.

Jean Warren

LANGUAGE IDEA

Make up a story about a sponge that loves to clean various items. Use a real sponge as a prop when you tell the story to your children.

SNACK IDEA

Let your children use damp sponges to wipe off the table before and after snacktime.

Paper Towels

Painting on Paper Towels

For each of your children, tape a plain white paper towel to a tabletop. In small containers, mix drops of food coloring with water. Give your children brushes and let them paint the colored water on their paper towels. When the towels have dried, mount them on sheets of colored construction paper to display on a wall.

MOVEMENT

Rolling, Rolling

Let your children lie on the floor, pretending to be wound-up rolls of paper towels. Have them roll across the floor in one direction to "unwind." Then have them roll back across the floor to "wind up" again.

RHYME

Cleaning Up Drips

Tearing off
Paper towels,
Zip, zip, zip.
Now my towels
Are ready
To clean up some drips.

Elizabeth McKinnon

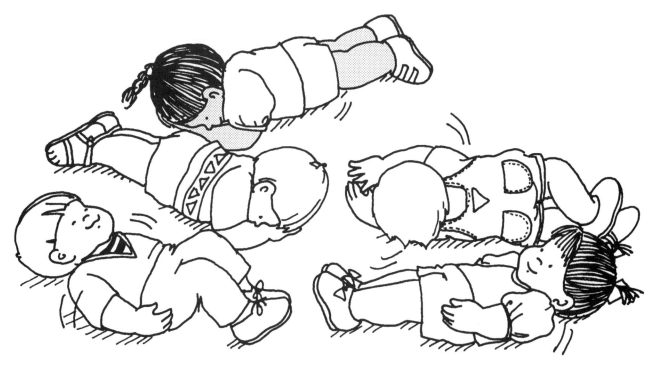

LANGUAGE IDEA

Cut familiar shapes out of thick, fluffy paper towels. Use the shapes on a flannelboard to tell a story to your children.

SNACK IDEA

Let your children use folded paper towels for napkins at snacktime.

SONG

With My Towel

Sung to: "If You're Happy and You Know It"

I am scrubbing
All the windows
With my towel.
I am scrubbing
All the windows
With my towel.
I am scrubbing
High and low.
I am scrubbing
Fast and slow.
I am scrubbing
All the windows
With my towel.

Repeat, each time substituting a different word, such as *tables* or *walls*, for *windows*.

Gayle Bittinger

Crackers

HANDS-ON LEARNING GAME

Cracker Match

Cut round, square, and triangular cracker shapes out of posterboard. Trace around the shapes on paper plates. Store the cracker shapes in cracker boxes that originally contained round, square, and triangular crackers, if desired. Give the cracker shapes and the paper plates to your children. Let them place the crackers on top of the matching shapes on the plates.

MOVEMENT

Be an Animal

Have your children stand in an open area. Hold up a box of animal crackers. As you take out one animal cracker at a time, have your children pretend to be that animal and act out its movements. Save the crackers to use for the Language Idea (page 47).

RHYME

Crackers

Crackers
Are snackers
That I love
To munch,
'Cause crackers
Are snackers
That make
A loud crunch!

Elizabeth McKinnon

Cracker Song

Sung to: "Down by the Station"

Out in
The kitchen,
When the clock
Says snacktime,
See the
Little crackers
Lined up
In a row.
See us add
Some cheese
Or creamy
Peanut butter.
Crunch, crunch,
Munch, munch.
Down they go!
   (Pretend to eat.)

Elizabeth McKinnon

Eating Crackers

Sung to: "Frere Jacques"

Eating crackers,
Eating crackers
For my lunch,
For my lunch.
Little round crackers,
Little square crackers.
Crunch, crunch, crunch.
Munch, munch, munch.

Elizabeth McKinnon

LANGUAGE IDEA

Set out different kinds of crackers for your children to sample. Ask them to describe the different tastes, textures, appearances, and shapes.

SNACK IDEA

Use crackers instead of bread to make peanut butter or cheese sandwiches.

JULY

Picnic Fun

HANDS-ON DRAMATIC PLAY

Picnic Play

In a picnic basket, place items such as a tablecloth, napkins, plates, cups, and spoons. Also add a few empty food containers such as yogurt cups or mustard and ketchup squeeze bottles. Let your children unpack the basket, have a pretend picnic, and then pack up the basket again.

MOVEMENT

Around the Basket

Stand with your children in a large circle. Place a picnic basket on the floor in the middle. Then move around the circle with the children as you sing the song "The Picnic Basket" (page 51).

RHYME

Picnic Basket

Picnic basket,
Open it wide.
What are some things
You see inside?

Chips and pickles,
Sandwiches, too.
A picnic lunch
For me and you.

Elizabeth McKinnon

Picnic in the Park

Sung to: "She'll Be Coming Round the Mountain"

Yes, we'll all go on
A picnic in the park.
Yes, we'll all go on
A picnic in the park.
Bring some lunch
And bring a ball.
There will be
Such fun for all!
Yes, we'll all go on
A picnic in the park.

Barbara Paxson

The Picnic Basket

Sung to: "The Mulberry Bush"

Here we go round
The picnic basket,
The picnic basket,
The picnic basket.
Here we go round
The picnic basket,
So early
In the morning.

Repeat, each time substituting a different action word, such as *skip, hop,* or *crawl,* for *go.*

Adapted Traditional

LANGUAGE IDEA

Tell your children a story about a picnic. As you do so, take items out of a picnic basket and use them as story props.

SNACK IDEA

Pack snack foods in a picnic basket and have an outdoor or an indoor picnic.

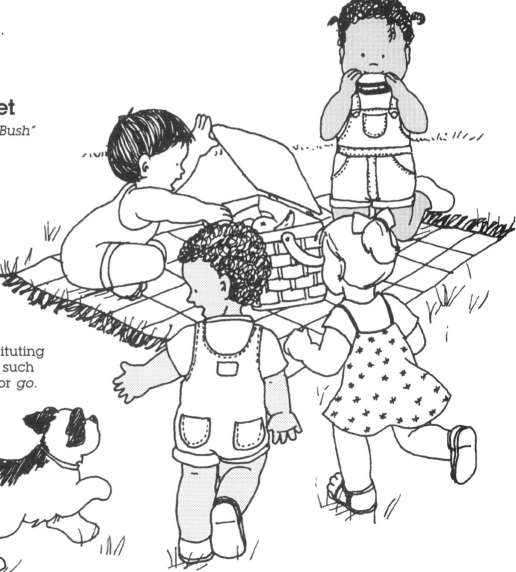

Paper Plates

HANDS-ON ART

Paper-Plate Lunches

Tear or cut pictures of nutritious foods out of magazines. Give each of your children a paper plate. Let the children brush glue on their plates. Then let them choose food pictures and place them on top of the glue. Display the plates on construction-paper "placemats," if desired.

MOVEMENT

Paper-Plate Toss

Collect several paper plates. Have your children stand in an open area. Give the plates to the children and have them see how far they can toss them.

RHYME

My Paper Plate

Have you seen
My paper plate,
Filled with
Things to eat?

Yes, I've seen
Your paper plate.
It's filled with
Cookie treats.

Repeat, each time substituting a different food name for *cookie*.

Elizabeth McKinnon

Paper Plates

Sung to: "Jingle Bells"

Paper plates,
Paper plates,
Fill them up
With treats.
Apples, oranges,
Sandwiches,
Oh, so good
To eat.
Paper plates,
Paper plates,
Add some
Pretzels, too.
See the plates
All filled up now,
Just for
Me and you.

Elizabeth McKinnon

LANGUAGE IDEA

Draw faces on paper plates and attach craft sticks for handles. Use the paper-plate puppets for telling stories.

SNACK IDEA

Serve each of your children a snack on a paper plate.

Ants

Observing Ants

Take your children on a walk to look for and observe ants. Or "invite" ants to come to you by placing a juicy piece of fruit outdoors on the ground. With the children, visit the site of the fruit after an hour or so to observe and talk about the ants that have discovered it. Remind your children to watch where they step so that they don't hurt the ants.

MOVEMENT

Scampering Ants

Have your children get down on their hands and knees, pretending to be little ants. Play music and let them crawl and scamper around on the floor. Whenever you stop the music, have the "ants" crawl under a table to hide in their "nest."

RHYME

Crawly Ant

See the little
Crawly ant
Walk across
The floor.
See the little
Crawly ant
Walk right to
The door.

See the little
Crawly ant
Creep out
In the sun.
Come again,
Crawly ant.
Watching you
Is fun!

Beverly Qualheim

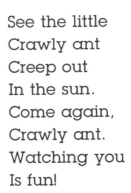

The Ants Are Busy

Sung to: "She'll Be Coming Round the Mountain"

Oh, the ants are busy,
Busy as can be.
Oh, the ants are busy,
Busy as can be.
See them scamper
Here and there,
See them scamper
Everywhere.
Oh, the ants are busy,
Busy as can be.

Oh, the ants are busy,
Busy as can be.
Oh, the ants are busy,
Busy as can be.
See them dig
And dig and dig
Lots of tunnels,
Oh, so big.
Oh, the ants are busy,
Busy as can be.

Kristine Wagoner

LANGUAGE IDEA

Make up a story about a hungry ant at a picnic. As you tell the story, let your children name foods that the ant wants to eat.

SNACK IDEA

Make "ants on logs" by filling short celery pieces with peanut butter and placing dark raisins on top.

Blankets

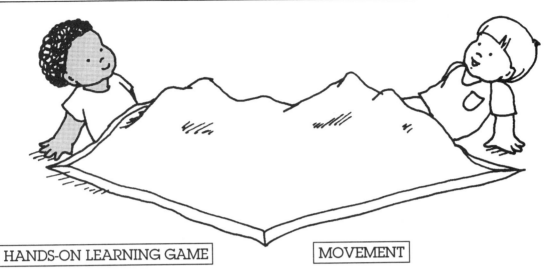

Blanket Peekaboo

Collect several familiar toys and a small blanket. As your children close their eyes, hide one of the toys under the blanket, leaving a small part of the toy exposed. Ask the children to open their eyes and try to guess which toy is under the blanket. Follow the same procedure with the rest of the toys.

MOVEMENT

Blanket Lift

Place a blanket on the floor. Have your children sit around the edges of the blanket and put their legs underneath it. When you give a signal, have all the children raise their legs at the same time to lift the blanket.

RHYME

I Once Had a Blanket

I once had a blanket
Fluffy and new,
And that little blanket
Was colored blue.

I once had a blanket
Soft as a pillow,
And that little blanket
Was colored yellow.

I once had a blanket
That just fit my bed,
And that little blanket
Was colored red.

Jean Warren

Beach Blanket Song

Sung to: "Down by the Station"

Down by the beach
Early in the morning,
See the pretty
Beach blankets
All in a row.
Here come the swimmers
To sit down
On their blankets.
Plop, plop, plop, plop.
Down they go.

As you sing the song, have your children pretend to be swimmers and act out the movements described.

Jean Warren

LANGUAGE IDEA

Invite your children to bring in their favorite blankets. Encourage them to talk about their blankets' sizes, colors, textures, and designs.

SNACK IDEA

Let your children sit on a blanket while they eat their snack.

Flags

Group Flag

Give each of your children a square of colorful construction paper. Let the children attach foil stars or other kinds of stickers to their squares. Then attach the children's papers in a flag shape to a wall and add a construction-paper flagpole.

MOVEMENT

Waving Flags

Make a "flag" for each of your children by attaching a rectangle of crepe paper to a cardboard paper-towel tube. Hand out the flags. Then have the children wave their flags as you give directions such as these: "Wave your flags high. Wave your flags low. Wave your flags back and forth. Wave your flags in circles."

RHYME

Wave Your Flags

Wave your flags,
Wave your flags
As you march
Around.
Wave your flags
High in the air.
Don't let them
Touch the ground!

JoAnn C. Leist

Marching Flags

Sung to: "When the Saints Go Marching In"

Oh, when the flags
Go marching by,
Oh, when the flags
Go marching by,
How we love to see
The colors
When the flags go
Marching by.

Jean Warren

LANGUAGE IDEA

Show your children an American flag. Talk about the colors, the stars, and the stripes.

SNACK IDEA

Write each of your children's names on a small paper rectangle. Attach each rectangle to a straw to make "flags" for snacktime drinks.

Stars

HANDS-ON ART

Night Sky Stars

Select a piece of white construction paper for each of your children. Use a white crayon to draw several stars on each paper. (Be sure to press down hard with the crayon when coloring in the stars.) Let your children brush thinned black tempera paint over their papers and watch as the stars appear in the "night sky."

RHYME

Wish on a Star

Star light,
Star bright,
First star
I see tonight.
I wish I may,
I wish I might
Have the wish
I wish tonight.

Traditional

MOVEMENT

Reach for the Stars

Cut star shapes out of yellow or white posterboard and hang them from the ceiling at different heights. Let your children take turns jumping up to touch the stars.

SONGS

Little Stars

Sung to: "Frere Jacques"

Little stars,
Little stars,
Way up high
In the sky.
I can see
Them sparkle.
I can see
Them twinkle.
Way up high
In the sky.

Elizabeth McKinnon

The Stars Are Shining Bright

Sung to: "The Farmer in the Dell"

The stars are
Shining bright.
See their
Twinkling light.
When you see
The sky at night,
The stars are
Shining bright.

Gayle Bittinger

LANGUAGE IDEA

Cover a cardboard star shape with foil. Pass the star around and let each of your children make a wish on it.

SNACK IDEA

Serve slices of star fruit or toast made with star-shaped cookie cutters.

Twinkle, Twinkle, Little Star

HANDS-ON ART

Twinkling Stars

Make paint pads by placing folded paper towels in shallow containers and pouring on small amounts of tempera paint. Let your children press star-shaped cookie cutters on the paint pads, then on pieces of construction paper to make star prints. While the paint is still wet, help the children sprinkle on glitter.

MOVEMENT

Twinkle Dancing

Have your children pretend to be stars. Attach star stickers to their fingertips. Then play music and let the children "twinkle" and dance around the room.

RHYME

Twinkle, Twinkle, Little Star

Twinkle, twinkle,
Little star.
How I wonder
What you are.
Up above the world
So high,
Like a diamond
In the sky!

Traditional

SONG

A Tiny Little Star

Sung to: "Little White Duck"

There's a tiny little star
Way up in the sky.
A tiny little star
Up so very high.
It twinkles brightly
Through the night.
But during the day
It is out of sight.
There's a tiny little star
Way up in the sky.
Tiny little star.

Jean Warren

LANGUAGE IDEA

Make a "little star" puppet. Use it for telling stories about what the star can see from "up above the world so high."

SNACK IDEA

For the snack table, decorate paper cups and construction-paper placemats with star stickers.

Flashlights

Exploring Flashlights

Collect several different kinds of flashlights, including an ordinary flashlight, a penlight, and a small squeeze-type flashlight. Invite one of your children at a time to sit with you and examine the flashlights. Show the child how to hold the different flashlights and turn them on and off.

MOVEMENT

Flashlight Hop

Dim the lights in your room and turn on a flashlight. As you "hop" the beam across the floor, let one of your children at a time try hopping onto it. Continue until everyone has had a turn.

RHYME

Our Flashlight

When it is dark,
As dark
Can be,
We turn on
Our flashlight
And then we can see!

Elizabeth McKinnon

SONG

Flash Your Light

Sung to: "Row, Row, Row Your Boat"

Flash, flash,
Flash your light.
Flash it
All around.
Flash it high.
Flash it low.
Flash it
On the ground.

Flash, flash,
Flash your light.
Flash it
Here and there.
Flash it high.
Flash it low.
Flash it
Everywhere.

Jean Warren

LANGUAGE IDEA

Dim the lights and tell your children a story by flashlight.

SNACK IDEA

Lead your children on a "hike" to the snack table by shining a flashlight on the floor as you walk.

Tents

HANDS-ON DRAMATIC PLAY

Tent Fun

Set up a real tent for your children. Or make a tent by draping a blanket or a sheet over a clothesline. Place a sleeping bag, a play flashlight, and some plastic dishes inside the tent and let your children take turns "camping out."

RHYME

Here Is My Tent

Here is my tent,
Cozy as can be.
Won't you come in
And play with me?

Elizabeth McKinnon

MOVEMENT

In and Out the Tent

Make a tent that is open at the front and back by draping a sheet or a blanket over a table. Let your children crawl in the front of the tent and out the back as you sing the song "In and Out the Tent" (page 67).

SONGS

Crawl Inside The Tent

Sung to: "Row, Row, Row Your Boat"

Let's crawl
Inside the tent.
Let's crawl
Inside today.
When we crawl
Inside the tent,
We can laugh
And play.

Elizabeth McKinnon

In and Out the Tent

Sung to: "Go In and Out the Window"

Go in and out the tent,
Go in and out the tent.
Go in and out the tent,
As we have done before.

Let your children go in and out
a real or a pretend tent while
singing the song.

Adapted Traditional

LANGUAGE IDEA

Sit inside a tent with your children
and read them a story.

SNACK IDEA

Let your children enjoy eating
their snack inside a tent.

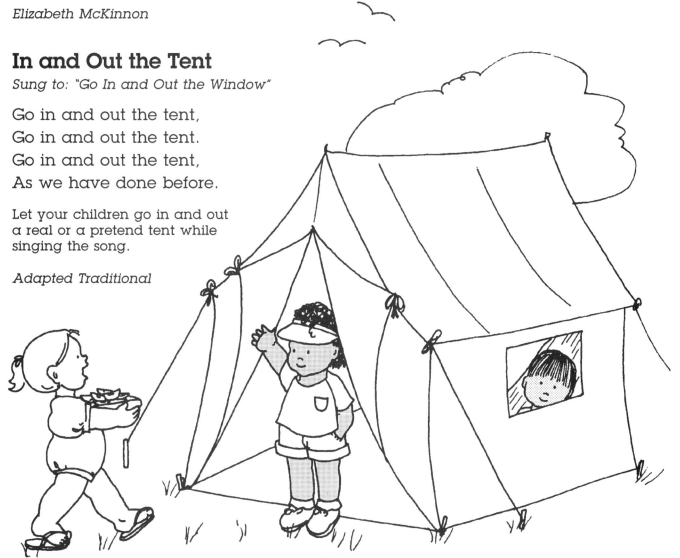

Books

MOVEMENT

Act It Out

Choose a storybook that has a lot of action such as *Caps for Sale* by Esphyr Slobodkina. Read the book to your children and let them act out the story.

HANDS-ON LEARNING GAME

Our Counting Book

Make a blank book by fastening five pieces of white paper together with a colored construction-paper cover. Write "Our Counting Book" on the front. Use a felt-tip marker to number the pages from 1 to 5. With your children, attach matching numbers of stickers to each page. Then give the book to the children to "read" to one another.

RHYME

My Book

Here is
My book.
I'll open
It wide
To show you
The pictures
That are
Inside.

Adapted Traditional

Take a Look

Sung to: "If You're Happy and You Know It"

Take a look,
Take a look
At my book.
Take a look,
Take a look
At my book.
Turn the pages
Nice and slow.
Look at pictures
As you go.
Take a look,
Take a look
At my book.

Elizabeth McKinnon

LANGUAGE IDEA

Sit with your children in the book corner. Talk with them about how to handle and take care of books.

SNACK IDEA

Read a favorite storybook to your children while they eat their snack.

Blue

Making Waves

Fill a small plastic jar two-thirds full with water. Add drops of blue food coloring. Then fill up the rest of the jar with mineral oil, eliminating as many air bubbles as possible. Screw on the jar lid and secure it with tape. Let your children hold the jar horizontally and gently tip it back and forth to create blue "waves."

RHYME

Use Your Eyes

Use your eyes.
Use your eyes.
You can look and see.
If you have on
Blue shirts,
Come and stand by me.

Repeat, each time substituting a different word, such as *pants*, *shoes*, or *jackets*, for *shirts*.

Adapted Traditional

MOVEMENT

Blue Rain

Cut blue crepe-paper streamers into long strips and hang them from the ceiling. Let your children walk or run through the "rain."

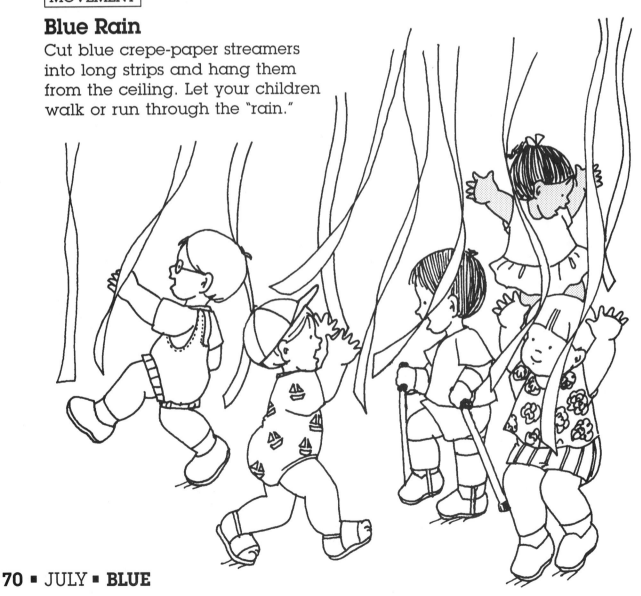

Jessie Wore Her Blue Dress

Sung to: "Did You Ever See a Lassie?"

Oh, Jessie wore
Her blue dress,
Her blue dress,
Her blue dress.
Oh, Jessie wore
Her blue dress
To school today.
Her blue dress,
Her blue dress.
Her blue dress,
Her blue dress.
Oh, Jessie wore
Her blue dress
To school today.

Sing the song for each of your children, naming a blue item of clothing that he or she is wearing.

Traditional

Blue

Sung to: "Three Blind Mice"

Blue, blue, blue.
Blue, blue, blue.
What is blue?
What is blue?
The sea, the sky,
And some people's eyes.
Blueberries picked
For a scrumptious pie.
A bluebird flying
Way up high.
They all are blue.

Diane Thom

Make up a blue story and illustrate it with a blue felt-tip marker as you tell it to your children.

Let your children decorate pieces of light-blue construction paper with blue stickers or blue crayon designs to make placemats for the snack table.

Little Boy Blue

HANDS-ON ART

Little Boy Blue Pictures

Make "straw" by cutting dried grass into short pieces. Let your children brush glue on pieces of construction paper and place the straw pieces on top of the glue to make "haystacks." Cut child shapes out of blue construction paper. Give one shape to each of your children to glue at the bottom of his or her haystack for Little Boy Blue.

MOVEMENT

Under the Haystacks

Have several pairs of children hold hands and raise their arms high to make "haystacks." Let the other children take the part of Little Boy Blue. Have them walk around as you play music. Whenever you stop the music, have them find haystacks and lie down under them. Then choose new children to form the haystacks and start the game again.

RHYME

Little Boy Blue

Little Boy Blue,
Come blow your horn.
The sheep's in the meadow,
The cow's in the corn.
But where is the boy
Who looks after the sheep?
He's under the haystack,
Fast asleep.

Traditional

Little Boy Blue Song

Sung to: "Twinkle, Twinkle, Little Star"

Little Boy Blue,
Come blow your horn.
> *(Pretend to blow horn.)*

The sheep's in the meadow,
The cow's in the corn.
> *(Point to right, then left.)*

But where is the boy
Who looks after the sheep?
> *(Look all around.)*

He's under the haystack,
Fast asleep.
> *(Pretend to sleep.)*

Little Boy Blue,
Come blow your horn.
> *(Pretend to blow horn.)*

The sheep's in the meadow,
The cow's in the corn.
> *(Point to right, then left.)*

Repeat, substituting *Little Girl Blue*
for *Little Boy Blue.*

Adapted Traditional

LANGUAGE IDEA

Ask your children to tell about
different places where they have
fallen asleep such as on the floor,
in a chair, or in someone's lap.

SNACK IDEA

Make blue gelatin to serve as a
"Little Boy Blue" snack.

Horns

Horn Sounds

Invite local musicians to come in and show what different kinds of horns look like and demonstrate how they sound. Or display pictures of horns for your children to observe as they listen to musical recordings that include horn passages.

MOVEMENT

Horn Parade

Collect one party horn for each of your children. Line up the children and hand out the horns. Then play music and let them parade around the room, tooting their horns as they march.

Variation: Let your children use cardboard tubes for horns.

RHYME

My Little Horn

Watch me play
My little horn.
I put my fingers so.
> (Place fists end to end.)

Then I lift it
To my mouth
And blow and blow and blow.
> (Bring fists to mouth and toot.)

Adapted Traditional

Toot Your Horn

Sung to: "If You're Happy and You Know It"

Toot your horn
In the air,
In the air.
Toot your horn
In the air,
In the air.
Toot your horn
In the air.
Make music
Everywhere!
Toot your horn
In the air,
In the air.

Jean Warren

Toot the Horns

Sung to: "London Bridge"

Toot the horns,
It's marching time,
Marching time,
Marching time.
Toot the horns,
It's marching time.
Toot, toot, toot!

Betty Silkunas

LANGUAGE IDEA

Tell a story about a horn. Whenever your children hear the word *horn*, have them make tooting sounds.

SNACK IDEA

Blow a horn to signal the beginning and end of snacktime.

Cows

Cow Match

Cut six identical cow shapes out of white posterboard. Divide them into three pairs. Use felt-tip markers to decorate each pair of cows differently. Then mix up the shapes and let your children take turns finding the matching cows.

MOVEMENT

Leading the Cows Home

With your children, pretend to be cows. Get down on all fours with the children behind you. Then lead them around the room, having them copy your movements, until you finally reach your big barn "home."

RHYME

Milk the Cow

Milk the cow,
Milk the cow
While sitting on a stool.
Pulling, squirting,
Pulling, squirting,
Till the bucket's full.

Pat Beck

SONG

What Do Cows Say?

Sung to: "London Bridge"

What do cows say?
Moo, moo, moo.
Moo, moo, moo.
Moo, moo, moo.
What do cows say?
Moo, moo, moo,
On the farm.

Cows eat grass and
Chew, chew, chew.
Chew, chew, chew.
Chew, chew, chew.
Cows eat grass and
Chew, chew, chew,
On the farm.

Additional verses: Cows give milk, that's true, true, true; I like milk, don't you, you, you?

Becky Valenick

LANGUAGE IDEA

Talk with your children about how cows give milk and how that milk is made into various dairy products.

SNACK IDEA

Serve dairy products such as milk, cheese, butter, yogurt, or ice cream.

Blueberries

Blueberry Paint

Place fresh blueberries in a shallow container. Let your children watch as you mash the berries with a fork and add a small amount of water to extend the juice. Then let the children use the juice to paint designs on pieces of white construction paper or paper towels. (Note: Have your children wear smocks to protect against blueberry stains.)

MOVEMENT

Little Blueberries

Have your children pretend to be blueberries growing on a big bush. As you walk around and "pick" the berries, have them jump into a big pretend bowl. Then let them act out the movements as you "wash" the berries and then "stir" them with pretend flour, milk, and sugar to make "blueberry muffins," "blueberry waffles," etc.

RHYME

Yum!

Here are
Blueberry muffins.
Here's a
Blueberry pie.
And here are
Blueberry pancakes,
Stacked on a plate
So high.
Yum!

Elizabeth McKinnon

SONG

The Blueberry Bush

Sung to: "The Mulberry Bush"

Here we go round
The blueberry bush,
The blueberry bush,
The blueberry bush.
Here we go round
The blueberry bush,
So early in the morning.

Pick the blueberries
Small and round,
Small and round,
Small and round.
Pick the blueberries
Small and round,
So early in the morning.

Now let's make some
Blueberry jam,
Blueberry jam,
Blueberry jam.
Now let's make some
Blueberry jam,
So early in the morning.

Repeat the last verse, each time
substituting a different word,
such as *pies, muffins, waffles,*
or *ice cream,* for *jam.*

Elizabeth McKinnon

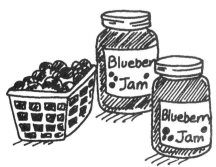

LANGUAGE IDEA

Let your children sample fresh
blueberries. Talk with them about
the color, shape, size, and taste of
the berries.

SNACK IDEA

Serve your children blueberry
muffins, blueberry pancakes, or
toast spread with blueberry jam.

Wheels

Counting Wheels

Collect various kinds of toys that have wheels such as cars, trucks, wheelbarrows, trikes, and wagons. Invite your children to sit with you. Encourage them to touch and examine the wheels on the toys. Then together count the number of wheels on each toy.

MOVEMENT

Parade on Wheels

Help your children decorate riding toys with crepe-paper streamers. Then let them ride the toys in a parade around the room or on a sidewalk outdoors.

RHYME

Watch the Wheels

Watch the wheels
Go round and round
As we drive
Our car to town.

Repeat, each time substituting a different word, such as *truck*, *van*, or *bus*, for *car*.

Judy Hall

Wheel Song

Sung to: "Old MacDonald Had a Farm"

Little Laura
Had a car.
E-I-E-I-O.
And on her car
She had some wheels.
E-I-E-I-O.
With a wheel,
Wheel here.
And a wheel,
Wheel there.
Here a wheel,
There a wheel,
Everywhere
A wheel, wheel.
Little Laura
Had a car.
E-I-E-I-O.

Sing the song for each of your children, substituting the child's name for *Laura* and the name of a different vehicle for *car*.

Jean Warren

LANGUAGE IDEA

Tell a story about wheels to your children. Have them roll their hands whenever they hear the word *wheels*.

SNACK IDEA

Place snack foods on a rolling cart and wheel them to the table to serve.

Cars

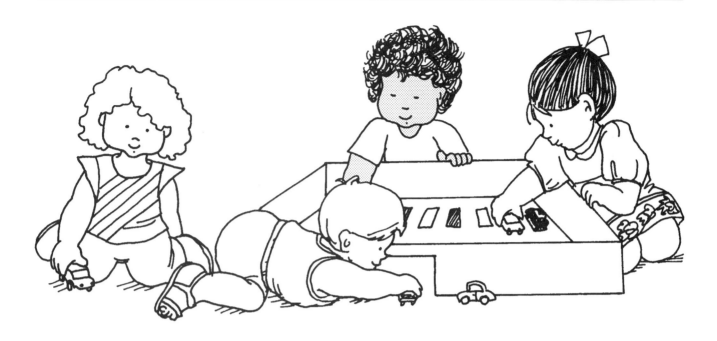

[HANDS-ON LEARNING GAME]

Color Parking

Collect several different colors of toy cars. Find a large shallow box to use for a parking garage. In the bottom of the box, draw or glue paper rectangles in colors that match the cars. Cut a square opening in one side of the box for a door. Let your children take turns driving the cars into the garage and "parking" them on the matching-colored rectangles.

[RHYME]

My Little Red Car

Hop aboard
My little red car.
    (Pretend to drive.)
Let's drive
Up and down.
Round and round
And round we go,
All around
The town.

Jean Warren

[MOVEMENT]

Toy Car Fun

Use strips of masking tape to make a race track on the floor. Give your children toy cars. Let them push the cars back and forth along the track, making putt-putt sounds as they go.

SONG

Riding in the Car

Sung to: "The Farmer in the Dell"

We're riding in the car.
We're riding in the car.
Heigh-ho, away we go.
We're riding in the car.

We're riding, oh, so far.
We're riding, oh, so far.
Heigh-ho, away we go.
We're riding, oh, so far.

Jean Warren

LANGUAGE IDEA

Sit with your children in a pretend car. Talk with them about what you see as you "drive" around.

SNACK IDEA

Set up a "restaurant" and let your children drive pretend cars to it for their snack.

Trucks

Truck Drivers

Have your children imagine that they are truck drivers. Let them climb into their pretend trucks and "drive" around the room. Periodically, hold up a red or a green circle to signal stop or go.

HANDS-ON DRAMATIC PLAY

Loading and Unloading

Collect several toy trucks. Use masking tape to create a large road map on the floor. Make sure that the roads are wide enough for the toy trucks to travel on. Set out materials such as wood blocks, small rocks, or toy logs. Let your children load the trucks with the materials and "drive" them to different locations on the road map for unloading.

RHYME

In My Truck

I am riding
In my truck.
Watch me
Going past.
I am riding
In my truck,
Going slow,
Then fast.

Gayle Bittinger

Truck Song

Sung to: "My Bonnie Lies Over the Ocean"

I love to ride
Down the highway.
Now I will
Tell you why.
I love to look
Out the window
And watch
The trucks go by.
Trucks, trucks,
Trucks, trucks.
I watch the trucks
Go by, go by.
Trucks, trucks,
Trucks, trucks.
I watch the trucks
Go by.

Jean Warren

Display pictures of cars and trucks. Talk with your children about how the vehicles are alike and how they are different.

Wrap snack foods in aluminum foil or plastic wrap. Place them in a large toy truck for delivering at snacktime.

Gas Station Fun

HANDS-ON DRAMATIC PLAY

Pumping Gas

Use a medium-sized cardboard carton to make a gas pump. Cut a small hole in the side of the carton. Cut off three or four feet of the end of an old garden hose. Insert the cut end of the hose into the hole in the carton and tape it securely in place. Attach a pistol-grip nozzle to the other end of the hose. Use felt-tip markers to add desired "gas pump" details to the box. Let your children take turns using the gas pump to "fill up" toy vehicles.

MOVEMENT

Car Wash

Make a Car Wash by cutting off the top and bottom of a large cardboard appliance box, laying the box on one side, and then hanging a row of fabric strips from the "ceiling" across the midpoint. Reinforce the box by wrapping tape around its sides, if necessary. Let your children take turns riding trikes into and out of the Car Wash.

RHYME

At the Gas Station

Hop in your car.
Take it for a ride.
Here's the gas station.
Drive inside.

Wash all the windows.
Put in some gas.
Then drive away,
But not too fast.

Adapted Traditional

SONG

A Gas Station

Sung to: "The Muffin Man"

Let's go find
A gas station,
A gas station,
A gas station.
Let's go find
A gas station.
Let's drive around
The block.

When we find
A gas station,
A gas station,
A gas station,
When we find
A gas station,
We'll slow right down
And stop.

Jean Warren

LANGUAGE IDEA

Tell your children a story about taking a car to a gas station. Include details about such things as pumping gas, adding oil, checking tires, and washing windows.

SNACK IDEA

Set up a pretend gas-station convenience store. Let your children "buy" snack foods with pretend money.

Wagons

Wagon Art

Cut pieces of white construction paper to fit inside a wagon. Place the paper in the wagon and add crayons or colored chalk. Let your children take turns standing or kneeling beside the wagon and drawing pictures on the paper inside it.

MOVEMENT

Wagon Parade

Let your children help decorate several wagons by taping on crepe-paper streamers and cutout paper shapes. Have the children place stuffed toys in the wagons. Then play music and let them push or pull the wagons around the room in a parade.

RHYME

My Wagon

I have a little wagon
I pull around with me.
I fill it with my toys
So everyone can see.

I love my little wagon.
Sometimes I jump inside,
Then I push with my two feet
And give my toys a ride.

Jean Warren

Wagon Ride

Sung to: "Ten Little Indians"

Hop aboard my
Little red wagon.
Hop aboard my
Little red wagon.
Hop aboard my
Little red wagon.
We'll ride around
The room.

Round and around
And around we go.
Round and around
And around we go.
Round and around
And around we go,
Round and around
The room.

Repeat, substituting *yard* or *block*
for *room*.

Jean Warren

As your children place toys inside
a wagon, make up a story about
the toys. At the end of the story,
have the toys go on a wagon ride.

Wrap snack foods in aluminum
foil or plastic wrap. Serve them
from a wagon pulled around the
snack table.

AUGUST

Dogs

In the Doghouse

Make a house for a toy dog
by turning a cardboard carton
upside down and cutting a
large door in one side. Place
the doghouse, along with the
toy dog, on the floor. Let your
children take turns playing with
the dog, moving it in and out of
its house. If desired, add a dog
dish and dog toys such as a ball
or a rawhide bone.

MOVEMENT

Puppy Moves

Let your children pretend to be
puppies. Recite the rhyme "Puppy,
Puppy" (this page). As you do so,
act out the movements and have
the children imitate you.

RHYME

Puppy, Puppy

Puppy, puppy,
Watch when
I say "Go!"
Puppy, puppy,
Wag your tail
Just so.

Repeat, each time substituting a different
phrase, such as *roll around, jump up
high,* or *sniff your nose,* for *wag your tail.*

Jean Warren

SONG

Three Little Puppy Dogs

Sung to: "Ten Little Indians"

One little, two little,
Three little puppy dogs.
One little, two little,
Three little puppy dogs.
One little, two little,
Three little puppy dogs
Bark like this all day.

    (Bark.)

Repeat, each time substituting a different word, such as *eat*, *sleep*, or *play*, for *bark*.

Carla Cotter Skjong

LANGUAGE IDEA

Hold up pictures of dogs and let your children make up names for them.

SNACK IDEA

Let your children bark once if they want juice, twice if they want a cracker, and so on.

Goldfish

Pet Goldfish

Bring in a goldfish, a fishbowl, aquarium gravel, and some aquarium plants. Let your children help set up the fishbowl for the goldfish. Place the bowl in a safe spot where the children can observe the fish swimming around in it. Encourage discussion of the parts of the fish and how it moves. If desired, let the children help with the feeding. (Note: Check with a pet store or an aquarium store for the proper way to set up your fishbowl and care for your fish.)

MOVEMENT

Swimming Fish

Arrange a long piece of yarn on the floor in a circle to represent a fishbowl. Let your children take turns pretending to be goldfish swimming around inside it.

RHYME

A Fishbowl

Kelsey has
A fishbowl.
In it is
A fish.
It swims
All around
With a swish,
Swish, swish.

Recite the rhyme for each of your children, substituting the child's name for *Kelsey*.

Adapted Traditional

I'm a Goldfish

Sung to: "Clementine"

I'm a goldfish,
I'm a goldfish.
See me wave
My fins like this.
> *(Wave arms at sides.)*

See me swim round
In my fishbowl.
> *(Move in a circle.)*

See my tail go
Swish, swish, swish.
> *(Wiggle hips.)*

Elizabeth McKinnon

LANGUAGE IDEA

Glue pictures of familiar objects onto goldfish shapes and place them in a glass bowl. Let your children take turns removing the shapes from the bowl and naming the objects pictured.

SNACK IDEA

Serve goldfish-shaped crackers that are made with orange Cheddar cheese.

Pet Care

HANDS-ON SCIENCE

Pet Day

Plan a Pet Day with your children. Invite them to bring in their pets—or photos of their pets—for others to see. Give each child a chance to talk about his or her pet and to tell how he or she helps care for it.

MOVEMENT

Pets and Owners

Have half your children pretend to be pet owners and let the other half pretend to be their pets. Have the owners do pretend activities such as feeding, walking, petting, and playing with their "pets." Then let the children reverse roles.

RHYME

Our Pet

Our pet has
A special place.
We keep it clean
And neat.
We feed our pet
Every day.
It sure likes
To eat!

Cindy Dingwall

Love Your Pets

Sung to: "Row, Row, Row Your Boat"

Love, love,
Love your pets,
Love them
Every day.
Give them food
And water, too.
Then let them
Run and play.

Elizabeth McKinnon

LANGUAGE IDEA

Using stuffed animals as props, talk with your children about the proper way to hold, pet, and play with pets.

SNACK IDEA

Use cookie cutters to cut toast into bone shapes for "doggy snacks" and fish shapes for "kitty snacks."

Animal Homes

Matching Game

On four pairs of index cards, draw or glue pictures of familiar animals and their homes. For example, on one pair of cards, draw a dog on one card and a doghouse on the other card. On another pair, draw a fish and a fishbowl. Mix up the cards. Then let your children take turns matching the pictures of the animals with the pictures of their homes.

MOVEMENT

Animals in Homes

Let your children act out different animals living in their homes such as bears in caves, rabbits in holes, cows in barns, squirrels in trees, or birds in nests.

RHYME

Houses

Here is a nest
For Mrs. Bluebird.
    (Cup hands together.)
Here is a hive
For Mr. Bee.
    (Place fists together.)
Here is a hole
For Mr. Rabbit.
    (Form circle with thumb and finger.)
And here is a house
For me.
    (Form roof shape with fingers.)

Adapted Traditional

Animal Homes

Sung to: "The Farmer in the Dell"

A squirrel
Lives in a tree.
A snail
Lives in a shell.
A bear lives
Inside a cave.
It suits her
Very well.

Repeat, each time substituting the name
of a different animal and its home, such
as *bird* and *nest* or *horse* and *barn*, for
bear and *cave*.

Elizabeth McKinnon

LANGUAGE IDEA

Make puppets by gluing pictures
of animals onto the ends of craft
sticks. Use the puppets for telling
stories about animals and their
homes.

SNACK IDEA

Let your children pretend to be
different animals and eat their
snack in their imaginary animal
homes.

Worms

Worm Collages

Cook whole-wheat spaghetti noodles as directed on the package. When they have cooled, use the brown noodles for "worms." Give each of your children a paper plate. Let the children arrange the noodles on their plates any way they wish to make Worm Collages. (The starch in the noodles will help the noodles stick to the plates when dry.)

MOVEMENT

Wiggle and Squirm

Have your children lie down on the floor in an open area. As you play music, have them wiggle and squirm like little worms.

RHYME

Wiggle Worm

One day when
I was playing,
I met a
Tiny worm.
Instead of
Going straight,
He squirmed and squirmed
And squirmed.

Here, now,
Let me show you
How he
Got around.
He wiggled,
Wiggled, wiggled
All across
The ground.

Jean Warren

LANGUAGE IDEA

Make a "worm puppet" by cutting a hole in the bottom of a paper cup and sticking a finger up through it. Use the puppet to tell your children a worm story.

SNACK IDEA

Let your children decorate placemats with "worm tracks" by dipping string into paint and dragging it across pieces of construction paper.

SONG

Little Worm

Sung to: "Twinkle, Twinkle, Little Star"

Slowly, slowly
Turn around.
Look behind you
On the ground.
You will see
A little worm.
Careful, now,
He'll make you squirm!
Slowly, slowly
Turn around.
There's a worm
Right on the ground.

Mildred Claus

The Sun

Sun Art

Give each of your children a yellow construction-paper circle for a sun. Set out 1-inch squares of yellow crepe paper or tissue paper. Let your children brush glue on their circles and place the paper squares on top of the glue. When the glue has dried, cut slits into the circles to make sun rays. Display the suns on a wall or a bulletin board, if desired.

MOVEMENT

Ring Around the Sun

Join hands with your children and walk in a circle as you sing the song below.

Sung to: "The Farmer in the Dell"

Oh, ring around the sun.
Oh, ring around the moon.
Oh, ring around
The great big world
As we sing this tune.

Jean Warren

RHYME

Bright Sun

Bright sun shining down,
    (Spread fingers and lower hands.)
Shining on the ground.
What a lovely face you have,
    (Form circle with arms.)
Yellow, big, and round!

Susan A. Miller

Sun Is Shining

Sung to: "Clementine"

Sun is shining,
Sun is shining,
Sun is shining
On the grass.
Sun is shining,
Sun is shining,
Sun is shining
On the grass.

Repeat, each time substituting a different word for *grass*.

Diane Thom

Talk with your children about fun things they can do in the sun.

Let your children sit outdoors in the sunshine and eat their snack.

Yellow

Yellow Match

Cut a large sun shape out of yellow posterboard or construction paper. Place the shape on a table or on the floor. Set out small yellow objects for your children to discover. When they do so, have them place the objects on top of the yellow sun shape.

MOVEMENT

Yellow Means Slow

Take your children outdoors and let them run around the play yard. Every now and then, hold up a circle cut from yellow construction paper. Whenever the children see the yellow circle, have them slow down.

RHYME

On My Pillow

I found
A little ribbon
Lying on
My pillow.
It was a
Pretty ribbon
And it was
Colored yellow.

Repeat, each time substituting a different word for *ribbon*.

Jean Warren

Stand Up for Yellow

Sung to: "London Bridge"

Kevin has a
Yellow shirt,
Yellow shirt,
Yellow shirt.
Kevin has a
Yellow shirt.
Stand up, Kevin.

Repeat for each of your children, substituting the name of the child for *Kevin* and the name of something yellow that the child is wearing or holding for *shirt*.

Elizabeth McKinnon

LANGUAGE IDEA

Look through a picture book with your children and have them name things they see that are yellow.

SNACK IDEA

Let your children help make lemonade for snacktime.

Corn

Corn on the Cob

Purchase several ears of fresh corn. Let your children help husk the corn and pull off the silk. (To remove stubborn silk strands, have the children rub the ears with dry paper towels.) When they have finished, cut the ears into short pieces and cook them in boiling water for 4 to 10 minutes or until tender. Cool before serving.

MOVEMENT

Growing Corn

Have your children bend down low as they plant pretend corn kernels in the ground in rows. When the "corn stalks" have grown tall, have the children stand on tiptoe and stretch their arms high to pick the pretend corn ears.

RHYME

Time for Corn

Juicy, tender
Yellow corn,
Ready on the plate.
Is it time
For dinner?
I can't wait!

Jean Warren

SONG

Munching on Sweet Corn

Sung to: "Skip to My Lou"

Standing in the
Corn field,
Out in the sun.
Picking the
Corn ears
One by one.
Cooking up the
Yellow corn,
Oh, what fun!
Munching on
Sweet corn,
Yum, yum, yum!

Jean Warren

LANGUAGE IDEA

Talk with your children about the parts of a corn plant, including the stalk, ears, husks, silk, kernels, and cobs.

SNACK IDEA

Let your children munch on their cooked corn sections from the activity Corn on the Cob (page 106). Or scrape the cooked kernels from the cobs and serve them in small bowls.

Vegetables

Veggie Match

On four pairs of index cards, draw or glue matching pictures of different vegetables such as tomatoes, corn, peas, and carrots. Mix up the cards and place them in a pile. Let your children take turns sorting through the cards to find the matching pairs.

MOVEMENT

Vegetable Soup

Form an imaginary soup pot by standing in a circle with your children. Give each child a picture of a vegetable. Pretend to stir the soup with a giant spoon. As you do so, name a vegetable and have the children who have a picture of that vegetable jump into the pretend soup pot and dance around as they "cook." Repeat until all the vegetables are in the soup pot.

RHYME

One Potato, Two Potato

One potato,
Two potato,
Three potato,
Four.
Five potato,
Six potato,
Seven potato
More.
Eight potato,
Nine potato,
Here is ten.
Now let's start
All over
Again.

Repeat, each time substituting a different vegetable name, such as *tomato* or *zucchini*, for *potato*.

Adapted Traditional

Out in the Garden

Sung to: "Down by the Station"

Out in the garden
Early in the morning,
See the red tomatoes
All in a row.
See the happy farmer
Coming out to pick them.
Pick, pick, pick, pick.
Off he goes.

Out in the garden
Early in the morning,
See the orange carrots
All in a row.
See the happy farmer
Coming out to pick them.
Pick, pick, pick, pick.
Off she goes.

Additional verses: See the yellow squashes; See the green string beans; See the purple cabbages.

Jean Warren

LANGUAGE IDEA

Set out a basket of fresh vegetables. As your children take turns removing the vegetables, name each one with the group.

SNACK IDEA

Serve fresh vegetables with a dip made by mixing plain yogurt with powdered salad dressing to taste.

Fruits

HANDS-ON COOKING

Making Fruit Salad

Let your children help prepare a fruit salad. Set out fruits such as bananas, oranges, apples, strawberries, and peaches. Have the children wash the fruit and help with the peeling. Let them use table knives to cut the fruit into bite-size pieces. Then have them help mix the pieces together in a large bowl.

MOVEMENT

Jammin'

Let your children dance around the room as you name different fruits. Occasionally, add the word jam to a fruit name. When you do so, have the children stamp their feet as if mashing the fruit into jam.

RHYME

Fruit Colors

There are many
Colored fruits.
They're so good
For you.
Apples are red;
Let's eat a few.
Bananas are yellow;
Let's try them, too.

Repeat, substituting other fruit names and colors for those in the rhyme.

Gayle Bittinger

SONG

Fruit Treats

Sung to: "Frere Jacques"

I'm a grape,
I'm a grape,
Growing on a vine,
Growing on a vine.
If you want
Some grape juice,
If you want
Some grape juice,
Smoosh me fine,
Smoosh me fine.

I'm a strawberry,
I'm a strawberry,
Growing on the ground,
Growing on the ground.
If you want
Some jam,
If you want
Some jam,
Mash me around,
Mash me around.

I'm an orange,
I'm an orange,
Growing on a tree,
Growing on a tree.
If you want
Some orange juice,
If you want
Some orange juice,
Just squeeze me,
Just squeeze me.

Polly Reedy

LANGUAGE IDEA

Decorate different fruits to make puppets and use them for telling stories to your children.

SNACK IDEA

Let your children enjoy their home-made fruit salad from the activity Making Fruit Salad (page 110). Serve in clear-plastic cups with a vanilla yogurt dressing.

The Circus

Circus Play

Let your children work together to make a "circus ring" by arranging a long piece of yarn in a circle on a carpet. When they have finished, give them toy animals and people to play with inside their ring.

MOVEMENT

Circus Acts

Make a "circus ring" on the floor with masking tape. Have your children pretend to be circus animals or performers while you play the part of ringmaster. Let them take turns entering the ring and performing as you announce such acts as prancing horses, parading elephants, roaring lions, dancing clowns, and tiptoeing tightrope walkers.

RHYME

At the Circus

At the circus
What do I see?
A great big elephant
Smiling at me.

Next to the elephant
What do I see?
A funny clown
Dancing for me.

Next to the clown
What do I see?
A little seal
Doing tricks for me.

Jean Warren

SONG

Circus Song

Sung to: "Mary Had a Little Lamb"

Let's all go to
The circus tent,
Circus tent,
Circus tent.
Let's all go to
The circus tent
To see what
We can see.

We will watch
The elephants march,
Elephants march,
Elephants march.
We will watch
The elephants march
Around the circus ring.

Additional verses: We will watch
the horses prance; We will watch the
dancing bears; We will watch the
clowns play tricks.

Jean Warren

LANGUAGE IDEA

Show pictures of circus acts
to your children. Let them
"announce" the acts by telling
what is happening in the pictures.

SNACK IDEA

Serve animal crackers that come
in boxes decorated like circus
train cars.

Clowns

Clown Hats

Let your children finger-paint
red designs on pieces of yellow
butcher paper. When the paint
has dried, cut the papers into
half-circles. Roll the half-circles
into cone-shaped hats and
tape the edges closed. Attach
pompons, cotton balls, or short
crepe-paper streamers to the tops
of the hats.

MOVEMENT

Clown Moves

Have your children pretend to be
clowns. Play circus music and let
them dance around the room,
making funny clown movements
and clown faces. Encourage them
to try to make one another laugh.

RHYME

Be a Clown

Be a clown, be a clown.
Be a funny clown.
> *(Wiggle fingers next to ears.)*
Juggle balls and jump rope.
> *(Pretend to juggle, then jump.)*
Then fall down on the ground.
> *(Sit down on bottom.)*

Diane Thom

SONGS

We Are Clowns Today

Sung to: "The Farmer in the Dell"

We are clowns today.
We are clowns today.
Heigh-ho, the derry-oh.
We are clowns today.

Additional verses: We do tricks today;
We make faces today; We fall down
today.

Paula C. Foreman

Funny Clowns

Sung to: "Frere Jacques"

Funny clowns,
Funny clowns
Jump around,
Jump around.
Sometimes
Making faces.
Sometimes
Running races.
Funny clowns,
Funny clowns.

Jean Warren

LANGUAGE IDEA

Use a toy clown as a puppet to
tell a story to your children.

SNACK IDEA

Let your children wear their hats
from the activity Clown Hats
(page 114) while they eat their
snack.

Elephants

MOVEMENT

Elephant Moves

Show your children how to hold their two arms together in front of their bodies and swing them back and forth like an elephant trunk. Then recite the rhyme "Elephant Walk" (this page) and have the children swing their "trunks" as they walk around the room.

HANDS-ON ART

Gray Painting

Pour gray tempera paint into shallow containers. Give each of your children a piece of white construction paper and a paintbrush. Let the children paint on their papers with the gray paint. When the papers have dried, cut them into elephant shapes, if desired.

RHYME

Elephant Walk

Right foot, left foot,
See me go.
I am gray and
Big and slow.
Watch me walking
Down the street
With my trunk
And four big feet.

Adapted Traditional

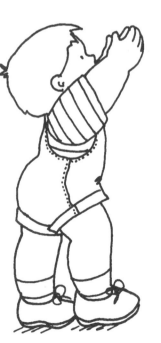

Who Is He?

Sung to: "Frere Jacques"

Big and slow.
Hear him go.
Oh, so huge,
Oh, so huge.
He makes a sound
Like thunder.
Who is he,
I wonder?
See his trunk.
Elephant!

Cynthia Walters

Big and Gray

Sung to: "The Mulberry Bush"

Elephants are
So big and gray,
Big and gray,
Big and gray.
Elephants swing
Their trunks this way,
Back and forth
All day.

Have your children use their arms as trunks and swing them back and forth as they sing.

Carla Cotter Skjong

LANGUAGE IDEA

Hold up a toy elephant or an elephant picture. As you point to the parts of the elephant, name them with your children.

SNACK IDEA

For a peanut snack, serve peanut butter spread on crackers or peanut butter sandwiches.

Monkeys

HANDS-ON LEARNING GAME

Banana Count

Cut a monkey shape out of brown felt and place it on a flannelboard. Cut 5 to 10 banana shapes out of yellow felt and put them in a pile. Let your children take turns "feeding the monkey" by placing banana shapes on the flannelboard. As they do so, count the bananas with the group.

MOVEMENT

Do What I Do

Let your children pretend to be monkeys. Make different movements and faces and have the "monkeys" imitate you. Then let the children pair up and take turns imitating their partners' faces and movements.

RHYME

I'm a Little Monkey

I'm a little monkey.
Watch me play,
   (Hop around.)
Munching on bananas
Every day.
   (Pretend to eat.)
I have monkey friends
Who play with me.
   (Point to others.)
See us climb
Right up the tree!
   (Pretend to climb.)

Carla Cotter Skjong

Monkey See, Monkey Do

Sung to: "Jingle Bells"

Monkey see,
Monkey do
Just the same
As you.
If you blink,
Then he will blink.
He likes to
Copy you.
Monkey see,
Monkey do
Just the same
As you.
If you blink,
Then he will blink.
He likes to
Copy you.

Repeat, each time substituting
a different action
word for *blink*.

Debra Lindahl

LANGUAGE IDEA

Make puppets by attaching monkey stickers or paper monkey shapes to the ends of craft sticks. Let your children use the puppets for telling stories.

SNACK IDEA

Give each of your children a banana half to peel and eat.

Beanbags

HANDS-ON LEARNING GAME

Beanbags for Playing

Make beanbags in various sizes and shapes, using fabric in a variety of colors, patterns, and textures. Fill the beanbags with large dried beans and stitch them securely closed. Let your children explore the beanbags. Talk with them about the different colors. Encourage the children to touch the beanbags and notice the different textures.

MOVEMENT

Beanbag Toss

Make a "target" by using felt-tip markers to draw a large clown face on a piece of butcher paper. Cut out the face and tape it to the floor. Let your children stand near the clown face and try to toss beanbags onto it.

Variation: Let your children try to toss beanbags into a laundry basket or a similar container.

RHYME

A Beanbag

Here is
A beanbag.
I'll toss
It to you.
Please catch it
And toss it
Right back
To me, too.

Adapted Traditional

SONG

Found a Beanbag

Sung to: "Clementine"

Found a beanbag,
Found a beanbag,
Found a beanbag
Just now.
Just now I
Found a beanbag,
Found a beanbag
Just now.

Picked it up,
Picked it up,
Picked it up
Just now.
Just now I
Picked it up,
Picked it up
Just now.

Tossed that beanbag,
Tossed that beanbag,
Tossed that beanbag
Just now.
Just now I
Tossed that beanbag,
Tossed that beanbag
Just now.

Adapted Traditional

LANGUAGE IDEA

Hand out beanbags to your children. Then give directions such as these: "Put your beanbag on the floor. Put your beanbag under a chair. Put your beanbag in this box."

SNACK IDEA

Let your children try to balance beanbags on their heads as they walk to the snack table.

Backyard Fun

Bell Ring

Hang a bell on a string from an outdoor clothesline or a tree branch. Give your children beanbags or rolled-up socks. Let them take turns tossing the beanbags or socks at the bell to try to make it ring.

RHYME

Our Yard

When it's time
To run and play,
Our yard is where
We go each day.

We smell the grass.
We hug the trees.
We listen to birds
And watch for bees.

Adapted Traditional

HANDS-ON DRAMATIC PLAY

Water Painting

Take your children out to the play yard. Give them buckets of water and large, clean paintbrushes. Let them dip the brushes into the water and then "paint" various surfaces around the yard such as fences, sides of buildings, or outdoor furniture.

SONG

Out in the Yard

Sung to: "Twinkle, Twinkle, Little Star"

Let's go out
In the yard and play.
The sun is shining,
It's a beautiful day.
We will hop
And skip and run,
And we'll have
A lot of fun.
Let's go out
In the yard and play.
The sun is shining,
It's a beautiful day.

Patricia Coyne

LANGUAGE IDEA

Find a nice spot in your play yard, such as under a tree or near a bush, and read a picture book to your children.

SNACK IDEA

Give each of your children a snack in a paper lunch bag to eat outdoors in the yard.

Jack and Jill

Jack and Jill Fun

Recite the rhyme "Jack and Jill" (this page). As you do so, have your children walk around the room, pretending to be Jack and Jill climbing a hill. When you get to the line that begins "Jack fell down," have the children drop to the floor and roll and tumble about.

HANDS-ON LEARNING GAME

A Pail of Water

Fill a large tub with water and add several plastic measuring cups. Give your children a small pail. Let them fill the measuring cups with water and then pour the water into the pail. Count with them the number of cups it takes to fill the pail. Help them empty the pail and then start the game again.

RHYME

Jack and Jill

Jack and Jill
Went up the hill
To fetch a pail
Of water.
Jack fell down
And broke his crown,
And Jill came
Tumbling after.

Traditional

Jack and Jill Song

Sung to: "Mary Had a Little Lamb"

Jack and Jill
Went up the hill,
Up the hill,
Up the hill.
 (Pretend to climb.)
Jack and Jill
Went up the hill
As high as
They could go.

Jack and Jill
Fell down the hill,
Down the hill,
Down the hill.
 (Tumble to floor.)
Jack and Jill
Fell down the hill,
Fell down,
Oh, so low.

Elizabeth McKinnon

LANGUAGE IDEA

Find a book of nursery rhymes. Read "Jack and Jill," along with other favorite rhymes, to your children.

SNACK IDEA

At snacktime, let your children help ladle water from a clean pail into small cups for drinking.

Up and Down

HANDS-ON LEARNING GAME

Up, Then Down

Sit with one or two of your children on the floor. Place several small toys or similar objects in front of you. Then give the children directions such as these: "Hold up the car. Put the car down. Hold up the block. Put the block down." Continue as long as interest lasts.

MOVEMENT

Up and Down

Take your children up and down stairs or a hill. Or let them toss balls or rolled-up socks up into the air and watch them come down.

RHYME

High and Low

Here's my little hand.
  (Hold out hand.)
Watch me make it go
First up so high,
  (Reach hand up.)
Then down so low.
  (Reach hand down.)

Repeat, each time substituting a different word, such as *block, toy,* or *crayon,* for *hand.*

Elizabeth McKinnon

Put Your Hands Up

Sung to: "Mary Had a Little Lamb"

Put your hands up to the sky,
To the sky, to the sky.
Put your hands up to the sky
And see if you can fly.

Put your hands down on the floor,
On the floor, on the floor.
Put your hands down on the floor
And try to count to four.

Linda Ferguson

See Us Reach Up

Sung to: "Here We Go Looby Loo"

See us reach
Up, up, up.
See us reach
Down, down, down.
See us reach
Up, up, up.
Now see us
Twirl all around.

Elizabeth McKinnon

Put a felt hill shape on a flannel-board. Let your children take turns placing other felt shapes up on top of the hill and down at the bottom.

At snacktime, have your children hold their hands up to request a snack item and put their hands down when they are served.

Swings

Swing Fun

Take your children to a play yard or a park that has swings. Let them take turns sitting in a swing as you gently push it back and forth.

RHYME

Swinging

Up and down,
Up and down
In the swing
Go I.
Up and down,
Up and down,
Swinging low,
Then high.

Jean Warren

HANDS-ON DRAMATIC PLAY

Toy Swing

Select a stuffed animal such as a bear or a rabbit. Attach yarn or ribbon to its arms or around its middle. Tie the yarn to a tree branch or a clothesline. Then let your children take turns pushing the stuffed toy back and forth.

SONG

I Am Swinging

Sung to: "Frere Jacques"

I am swinging,
I am swinging
Up so high,
Up so high.
First I swing
Forward,
Then I swing
Backward.
Touch the sky,
Touch the sky.

Susan Nydick

LANGUAGE IDEA

With your children, talk about swinging on a swing, including how it is done and how it feels.

SNACK IDEA

Have your children swing their arms up and down as they walk to the snack table.

Slides

Exploring Sliding

Stand with your children around
a small slide. One at a time,
place different items, such as
a stuffed animal, a ball, or a
sponge, at the top of the slide.
Ask your children to guess
whether the item will go down
the slide slowly or quickly. Then
let go of the item and have the
children observe what happens.

MOVEMENT

Sliding Fun

Take your children to a play yard
or a park where there is a small
slide. Let them take turns sliding
down the slide while you sing the
song "Sliding" (page 131).

RHYME

The Slide

Climb up the ladder.
> *(Climb fingers up arm.)*

Hang on to the side.
> *(Grasp arm with fingers.)*

Sit down at the top.
> *(Place fist at top of arm.)*

Then down you slide.
> *(Slide fist down arm.)*

Adapted Traditional

Sliding

Sung to: "Row, Row, Row Your Boat"

Climb, climb
Up the slide.
Climb up to
The top.
Sliding, sliding
Down the slide.
Slide until
You stop.

Elizabeth McKinnon

LANGUAGE IDEA

Talk with your children about slide safety tips such as these: Use only the ladder to get to the top of the slide. Slide down one at a time. Always slide down feet first.

SNACK IDEA

Let your children take turns sliding down a slide on their way to have their snack.

CHAPTER INDEX

BUSY BEES SERIES CHAPTER INDEX

Totline® Books

For parents, teachers, and others who work with young children

TEACHING THEMES

THEME-A-SAURUS®

Classroom-tested, around-the-curriculum activities organized into imaginative units. Great for implementing a child-directed program.

Theme-A-Saurus
Theme-A-Saurus II
Toddler Theme-A-Saurus
Alphabet Theme-A-Saurus
Nursery Rhyme Theme-A-Saurus
Storytime Theme-A-Saurus

BUSY BEES SERIES

Designed for two's and three's—these seasonal books help young children discover the world through their senses. Activity and learning ideas include simple songs, rhymes, snack ideas, movement activities, and art and science projects.

Busy Bees—SPRING
Busy Bees—SUMMER
Busy Bees—FALL
Busy Bees—WINTER

PLAY & LEARN SERIES

This creative, hands-on series explores the versatile play-and-learn opportunities of familiar objects.

Play & Learn with Stickers
Play & Learn with Paper Shapes and Borders
Play & Learn with Magnets
Play & Learn with Rubber Stamps
Play & Learn with Photos

GREAT BIG THEMES

Giant units that explore a specific theme through art, language, learning games, science, movement activities, music, and snack ideas. Includes reproducible theme alphabet cards and patterns.

Space
Farm
Zoo
Circus

CELEBRATIONS SERIES

Easy, practical ideas for celebrating holidays and special days around the world. Plus ideas for making ordinary days special.

Small World Celebrations
Special Day Celebrations
Great Big Holiday Celebrations

EXPLORING SERIES

Encourage exploration with hands-on activities that emphasize all the curriculum areas.

Exploring Sand and the Desert
Exploring Water and the Ocean
Exploring Wood and the Forest

NUTRITION

SNACKS SERIES

This series provides easy and educational recipes for healthful, delicious eating and additional opportunities for learning.

Super Snacks
Healthy Snacks
Teaching Snacks
Multicultural Snacks

LANGUAGE

CUT & TELL CUTOUTS

Each cutout folder includes a delightful tale, color figures for turning into manipulatives, and reproducible activity pages.

COLOR RHYMES *Rhymes and activities to teach color concepts.*

Cobbler, Cobbler
Hickety, Pickety
Mary, Mary, Quite Contrary
The Mulberry Bush
The Muffin Man
The Three Little Kittens

NUMBER RHYMES *Emphasize numbers and counting.*

Hickory, Dickory Dock
Humpty Dumpty
1, 2, Buckle My Shoe
Old Mother Hubbard
Rabbit, Rabbit, Carrot Eater
Twinkle, Twinkle, Little Star

NURSERY TALES *Enhance language development with these classic favorites.*

The Gingerbread Kid
Henny Penny
The Three Bears
The Three Billy Goats Gruff
Little Red Riding Hood
The Three Little Pigs
The Big, Big Carrot
The Country Mouse and the City Mouse
The Elves & the Shoemaker
The Hare and the Tortoise
The Little Red Hen
Stone Soup

TAKE-HOME RHYME BOOKS SERIES

Make prereading books for young children with these reproducible stories. Great confidence builders!

Alphabet & Number Rhymes
Color, Shape & Season Rhymes
Object Rhymes
Animal Rhymes

MUSIC

PIGGYBACK® SONGS

New songs sung to the tunes of childhood favorites. No music to read! Easy for adults and children to learn. Chorded for guitar or autoharp.

Piggyback Songs
More Piggyback Songs
Piggyback Songs for Infants & Toddlers
Piggyback Songs in Praise of God
Piggyback Songs in Praise of Jesus
Holiday Piggyback Songs
Animal Piggyback Songs
Piggyback Songs for School
Piggyback Songs to Sign
Spanish Piggyback Songs
More Piggyback Songs for School

BEAR HUGS® SERIES

Think you can't make it through another day? Give yourself a Bear Hug! This unique series focuses on positive behavior in young children and how to encourage it on a group and individual level.

Meals and Snacks

Cleanup

Nap Time

Remembering the Rules

Staying in Line

Circle Time

Transition Times

Time Out

Saying Goodbye

Saving the Earth

Getting Along

Fostering Self-Esteem

Being Afraid

Being Responsible

Being Healthy

Welcoming Children

Accepting Change

Respecting Others

1001 SERIES

These super reference books are filled with just the right tip, prop, or poem for your projects.

1001 Teaching Props

1001 Teaching Tips

1001 Rhymes & Fingerplays

THE BEST OF TOTLINE®

A collection of the best ideas from more than a decade's worth of Totline Newsletters. Month-by-month resource guides include instant, hands-on ideas for around-the-curriculum activities. 400 pages

LEARNING & CARING ABOUT SERIES

Developmentally appropriate activities to help children explore, understand, and appreciate the world around them. Includes reproducible parent flyers.

Our World

Our Selves

Our Town

MIX AND MATCH PATTERNS

Simple patterns, each printed in four sizes.

Animal Patterns

Everyday Patterns

Nature Patterns

Holiday Patterns

1•2•3 SERIES

Open-ended, age-appropriate, cooperative, and no-lose experiences for working with preschool children.

1•2•3 Art

1•2•3 Games

1•2•3 Colors

1•2•3 Puppets

1•2•3 Reading & Writing

1•2•3 Rhymes, Stories & Songs

1•2•3 Math

1•2•3 Science

1•2•3 Shapes

101 TIPS FOR DIRECTORS

Great ideas for managing a preschool or daycare! These hassle-free, handy hints help directors juggle the many hats they wear.

Staff and Parent Self-Esteem

Parent Communication

Health and Safety

Marketing Your Center

Resources for You and Your Center

Child Development Training

FOUR SEASONS SERIES

Each book in this delightful series provides fun, hands-on activity ideas for each season of the year.

Four Seasons–Movement

Four Seasons–Science

PARENTING RESOURCES

A YEAR OF FUN

These age-specific books provide information about how young children are growing and changing and what parents can do to lay a strong foundation for later learning. Calendarlike pages, designed to be displayed, offer developmentally appropriate activity suggestions for each month—plus practical parenting advice!

Just for Babies

Just for One's

Just for Two's

Just for Three's

Just for Four's

Just for Five's

TEACHING HOUSE SERIES

This new series helps parents become aware of the everyday opportunities for teaching their children. The tools for learning are all around the house and everywhere you go. Easy-to-follow directions for using ordinary materials combine family fun with learning.

Teaching House

Teaching Town

Teaching Trips

CHILDREN'S STORIES

Totline's children's stories are called Teaching Tales because they are two books in one—a storybook and an activity book with fun ideas to expand upon the themes of the story. Perfect for a variety of ages. Each book is written by Jean Warren.

Kids Celebrate the Alphabet

Ellie the Evergreen

The Wishing Fish

The Bear and the Mountain

HUFF AND PUFF® AROUND THE YEAR SERIES

Huff and Puff are two endearing, childlike clouds that will take your children on a new learning adventure each month.

Huff and Puff's Snowy Day

Huff and Puff on Groundhog Day

Huff and Puff's Hat Relay

Huff and Puff's April Showers

Huff and Puff's Hawaiian Rainbow

Huff and Puff Go to Camp

Huff and Puff on Fourth of July

Huff and Puff Around the World

Huff and Puff Go to School

Huff and Puff on Halloween

Huff and Puff on Thanksgiving

Huff and Puff's Foggy Christmas

Totline Books are available at local parent and teacher stores

Instant, hands-on activity ideas for working with young children

Totline® Newsletter

This newsletter offers creative hands-on activities that are designed to be challenging for children ages 2 to 6, yet easy for teachers and parents to do. Minimal preparation time is needed to make maximum use of common, inexpensive materials. Each bimonthly issue includes seasonal fun plus • learning games • open-ended art • music and movement • language activities • science fun • reproducible teaching aids • reproducible parent-flyer pages and • toddler activities. *Totline Newsletter* is perfect for use with an antibias curriculum or to emphasize multicultural values in a home environment.

Reproducible!

Super Snack News

This newsletter is designed to be reproduced!

With each subscription you are permitted to make up to 200 copies per issue! They make great handouts for parents. Inside this monthly, four-page newsletter are healthy recipes and nutrition tips, plus related songs and activities for young children. Also provided are category guidelines for the Child and Adult Care Food Program (CACFP). Sharing *Super Snack News* is a wonderful way to help promote parent involvement in quality childcare.